Joe Rogan

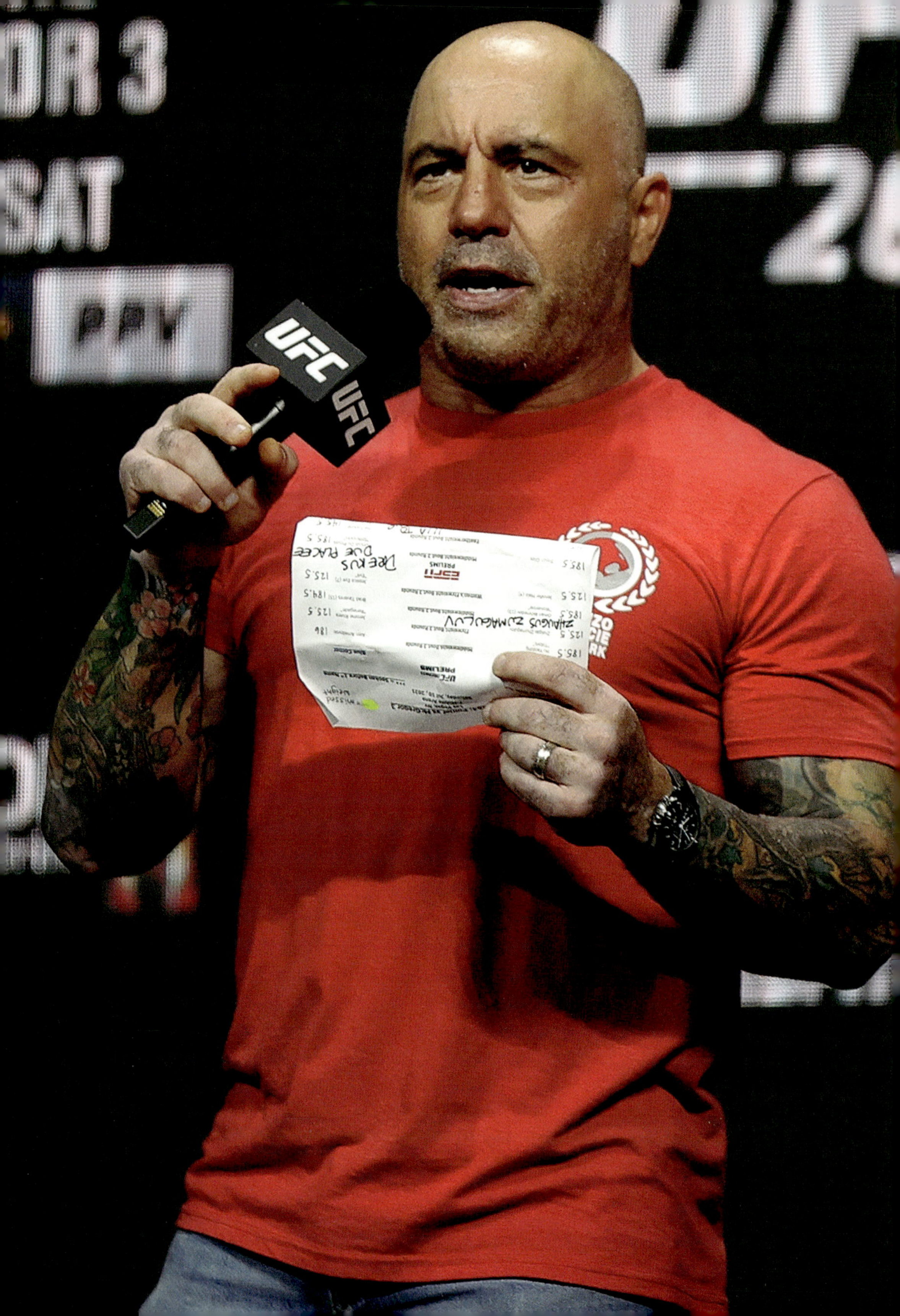
UFC
SAT
PPV

Joe Rogan

UFC ANNOUNCER AND POLITICAL PODCASTER

Mari Bolte

LERNER PUBLICATIONS ◆ MINNEAPOLIS

Lerner Publications Company
An imprint of Lerner Publishing Group, Inc.
241 First Avenue North
Minneapolis, MN 55401 USA

For reading levels and more information, look up this title at www.lernerbooks.com.

Main body text set in Rotis Serif Std 55 Regular. Typeface provided by Adobe Systems.

Library of Congress Cataloging-in-Publication Data

Names: Bolte, Mari, author.
Title: Joe Rogan : UFC announcer and political podcaster / Mari Bolte.
Description: Minneapolis : Lerner Publications , 2026. | Series: Gateway biographies | Includes bibliographical references and index. | Audience: Ages 9–14 | Audience: Grades 4–6 | Summary: "Joe Rogan began his career as a stand-up comedian and later hosted reality TV shows before becoming a UFC announcer and a podcaster. Learn about his life and the influence of his podcast"—Provided by publisher.
Identifiers: LCCN 2025003718 (print) | LCCN 2025003719 (ebook) | ISBN 9798765690550 (library binding) | ISBN 9798765690611 (paperback) | ISBN 9798765690642 (epub)
Subjects: LCSH: Rogan, Joe, 1967– | Internet personalities—United States—Juvenile literature. | Podcasters—United States—Biography—Juvenile literature. | Sportscasters—United States—Biography—Juvenile literature. | Comedians—United States—Biography—Juvenile literature. | LCGFT: Biographies.
Classification: LCC PN4587.2.R63 B65 2025 (print) | LCC PN4587.2.R63 (ebook) | DDC 791.46092 [B]—dc23/eng/20250131

LC record available at https://lccn.loc.gov/2025003718
LC ebook record available at https://lccn.loc.gov/2025003719

Manufactured in the United States of America
1 - CG - 7/15/25

TABLE OF CONTENTS

Joe Rogan's podcast has a significant impact on society, both inspiring listeners and creating controversy.

On October 25, 2024, Republican presidential nominee Donald Trump sat down at a state-of-the-art recording studio in Austin, Texas. Election day was less than a week and a half away. People expected him to be on the road, giving speeches in swing states to convince Americans to cast their votes for him. Trump had a rally in Michigan scheduled later that day. But instead of getting there early, he was settling in to do a podcast well-known for its long length.

"All right, we're rolling," the host said, leaning forward to speak into his microphone. He was sitting in front of a huge neon sign bearing the podcast's name: *The Joe Rogan Experience*. Trump smiled. The experience was about to begin.

Trump's interview with podcast host Joe Rogan lasted nearly three hours. The two talked about a wide range of topics, including wind turbines, the 2020 election, immigration, and foreign policy. Rogan let Trump steer the conversation, peppering in praises and, occasionally,

Donald Trump was sworn in as president for the second time on January 20, 2025.

pointed pushback. Rogan asked about hot-button issues like tariffs and election fraud and pressed Trump about subjects of personal interest, such as the environment and fair working conditions. At the end of the interview, Trump promised to come back for another. "You are a fascinating guy," Trump told Rogan before heading out.

Two years prior Rogan had refused to have Trump on his popular podcast. However, an assassination attempt on the presidential candidate in July 2024 convinced Rogan that it was time to extend an invite. Never one to shy away from controversy, he knew talking to Trump would thrill his listeners—and it did. The interview had thirty-eight million views on YouTube in just three days, with

Rogan gaining four hundred thousand new subscribers. His numbers on the social media platforms Instagram and X increased as well. Trump's running mate, J. D. Vance, would appear on Rogan's podcast a week later. In total, the audience for both interviews rivaled the number of people who watched the June 2024 debate between Trump and Democratic nominee Joe Biden.

Donald Trump went on to win the 2024 presidential election. Rogan's sway with Americans was undeniable. He could get interviews with the most powerful people in the nation—without having to leave his home—because they knew the importance of Rogan's audience. "Rogan now wields an unparalleled level of sway in a fracturing media environment," *Politico* writer Adam Wren wrote. And his influence would only continue to grow.

EARLY LIFE

Joseph James Rogan was born in Newark, New Jersey, on August 11, 1967. He has one younger sister, Laura. His parents, Susan and Joe Sr., divorced when he was five years old. Rogan has claimed that his father was physically and emotionally abusive. "The only thing my dad ever taught me was to not be like him," Rogan said later. Two years after the divorce, Susan, Joe, and Laura moved to San Francisco, California. It was the last time Rogan spoke to his father.

Susan remarried, and eventually the family moved to a suburb of Boston, Massachusetts. At school, Rogan

The 2024 Election

The 2024 presidential election was a historic one. Donald Trump had won in 2016 but lost in 2020. For months, Americans thought the 2024 election would be between Trump and incumbent President Joe Biden. But then, on July 21, 2024, Biden made an announcement–he would not run. Instead, he endorsed his vice president, Kamala Harris, for the position. Harris's win would have broken a number of records. She would have been the first woman president, as well as the first Black and Indian president.

Rogan (*center*) speaks with Donald Trump (*right*) and commentator Daniel Cormier at a UFC event in November 2024.

Voters went in a different direction, though. Trump won both the Electoral College and the popular vote, despite being the first former president convicted of felony crimes. The Electoral College is a body of people representing the United States. A president needs 270 out of 538 Electoral College votes to win. The popular vote is made up of regular citizens who cast their ballots. A candidate can win the popular vote and still lose the election.

Trump had survived two assassination attempts, which seemed to reenergize him. With the help of his eighteen-year-old son, Barron, Trump had turned to influential male podcasters to get the word out about his campaign. Besides *The Joe Rogan Experience*, Trump was a guest on other podcasts with a strong young, white male following. The appearances convinced many undecided voters that the candidate had their best interests in mind.

Rogan and his family eventually settled in Newton Upper Falls, a suburb of Boston.

felt like an outcast. He was small for his age, and the family had moved a lot. Rogan was always the new kid, and it made him feel insecure. But he never wanted to look weak. He thought learning how to fight would help his confidence. When he was fourteen, he started karate and then moved to tae kwon do. He worked hard, earning black belts and awards. He even started teaching classes.

During a match when Rogan was nineteen, he landed a kick that knocked his opponent out cold. The other fighter was taken out on a stretcher, leaving Rogan afraid that he had killed him. Rogan fought again that day and lost. He began worrying about getting hurt himself. With his enthusiasm gone, Rogan quit the sport. Rogan also enrolled in college at the University of Massachusetts,

Boston, but left before graduating. Something else had caught his attention.

While living in Boston, Rogan began buying cassette tapes of comedians' stand-up shows recorded at Redd Foxx's comedy club. He connected with comedian Richard Pryor's honest, explorative, organic stage presence. Rogan had used humor at martial arts tournaments to cut the tension before fights, and his friends encouraged him to try it out in front of other people.

In 1988 twenty-one-year-old Rogan did his first stand-up show at an amateur open mic night. He met local comics and tried out new jokes. Two years later he visited Los Angeles, California. He stopped at the world-famous Comedy Store, the club where professional funny people like Eddic Murphy, Robin Williams, and Steve

Many famous comedians got their start at The Comedy Store in Los Angeles.

Rogan performs a stand-up act at The Comedy Store in 2003.

Martin would practice new material. Just being in their shadows inspired Rogan.

Later that year he moved to New York City, hoping to get discovered by a celebrity, an agent, or anyone else who could boost his career. At first he barely made enough money to survive. He stayed with family members and took part-time jobs to pay the bills. Finally, near the end of the decade, talent agent Jeff Sussman saw one of Rogan's sets at an open-mic night and signed him immediately.

ROGAN ON TV

In 1993 a looming professional baseball strike made TV network executives realize they would need something to replace Major League Baseball (MLB) games on TV. Fox's solution was a sitcom called *Hardball*, which was about a

Royce Gracie (*right*) fights against Gerard Gordeau in the first UFC Championship in 1993.

fictional professional baseball team and its players. Rogan was cast as Frank Valente, an arrogant star pitcher who liked to stir up trouble. Rogan hoped the show would give him name recognition and further his stand-up career. Unfortunately, *Hardball* only lasted nine episodes. It struggled to find an audience in the prime time Sunday night spot that should have hosted the 1994 MLB season.

After *Hardball* was canceled, Rogan's schedule didn't stay quiet for long. His next gig was on a sitcom called *NewsRadio*. He played Joe Garrelli, a lovable, conspiracy-theory-loving handyman. It was his big break, and the show ran from 1995 to 1999.

Around this time, the Ultimate Fighting Championship (UFC) began to get popular. Founded in 1993, the UFC pitted athletes in various martial arts and other combat

The 1994–1995 MLB Strike

Toward the end of 1993 MLB owners and players found themselves in a disagreement. Over the past two decades players had fought for higher salaries and more freedom to choose where they played. Their union was incredibly powerful, and tensions between team owners and players were rising.

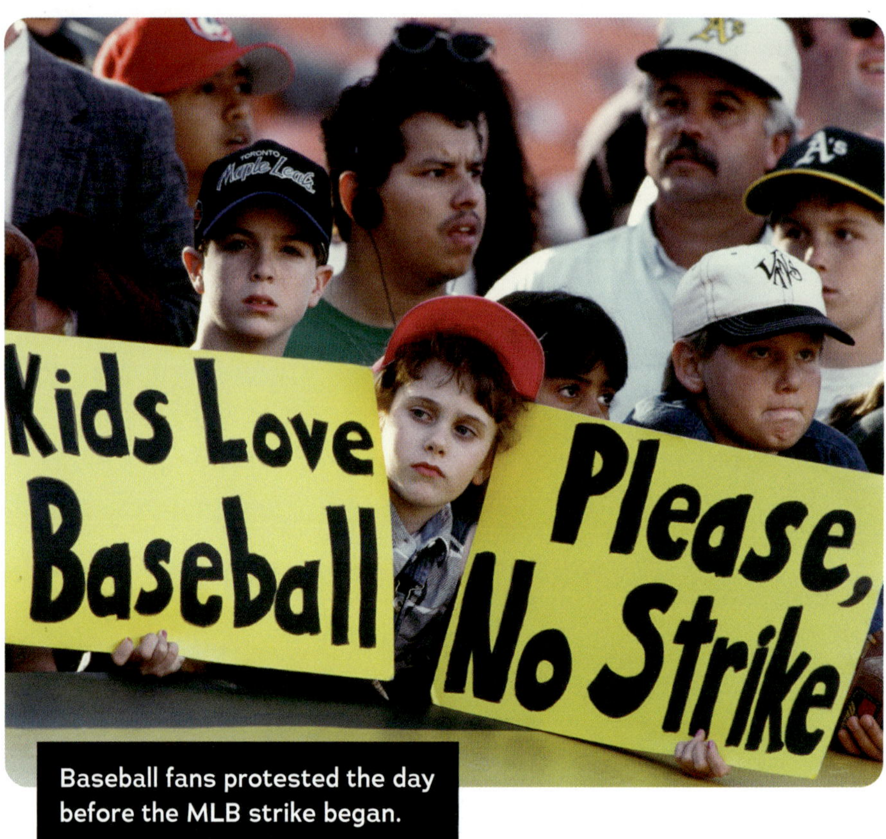

Baseball fans protested the day before the MLB strike began.

There was also inequality amongst the teams. Clubs with larger budgets like the New York Yankees and the Atlanta Braves were able to attract the best players with big paychecks. Smaller clubs proposed a revenue-sharing system, where higher-earning teams would share money to even things out. Higher-earning teams suggested players be paid partially from ticket sales and TV broadcasting fees. In addition, they worked to take away the players' negotiating power and their ability to change teams. The owners insisted this would be good for the players, but when players asked for more detailed information on how the plan would work, owners refused to share.

On August 12, 1994, the players went on strike. Some unproductive negotiations occurred, with neither side willing to give in. In total the strike lasted 232 days, officially ending on April 2, 1995. A new deal wasn't signed until November 1996. Both the 1994 and 1995 seasons were affected, with 948 canceled games. It was the first time the World Series had ever been canceled. Millions of dollars of revenue had been lost, and even more important, once-loyal fans stopped coming to games. Others showed up to boo the teams. They threw souvenir baseballs, flags, and other debris from the stands. During one game, they even stormed the field.

Rogan (*left*) and UFC president and CEO Dana White speak at an award show in 2006.

sports against each other, tournament-style, to find the ultimate fighting champion that night. Rogan jumped at the chance to get close to martial arts again. He began as a post-fight interviewer, talking to competitors after matches. It didn't pay well, though. At that point, the UFC was spending more money than it had, and there wasn't much left to pay employees. Rogan had to find his own way to matches, which were sometimes in rural, remote areas, and it cost him more money than he made. He quit after two years, although he remained a fan.

In 2001 the UFC was purchased by a new company who put on UFC fights in Vegas. He met Dana White, the CEO of UFC, who talked Rogan into returning as a color commentator in 2002. Color commentators describe what's going on to the audience during the fight and provide any necessary background information. "I didn't have any training at all in sports commentary," Rogan said. "I just would see what was happening and start talking about it." Despite his lack of training, Rogan's commentary style appealed to the fans. He was named the Fighters Only MMA Awards Show's MMA Personality of the Year eleven times between 2010 and 2024.

Rogan also continued his stand-up career, performing at The Comedy Store in Hollywood. He recorded his first

Rogan has won the MMA Personality of the Year award many times for his popular commentary.

stand-up comedy show in 1999. The show, called *I'm Gonna Be Dead Someday*, came out the following year. He had signed a deal for two more albums and was also planning a sitcom called *The Joe Rogan Show*. The sitcom was put on hold, though, because of Rogan's next job.

HOLLYWOOD REALITY

In 2000 a reality show called *Survivor* changed how people watched television. Other TV networks scurried to embrace reality television and copy this success. Soon, one of NBC's most popular shows was called *Fear Factor*.

Rogan celebrates *Fear Factor's* one hundredth episode in 2004.

Reality TV

Reality entertainment might seem like a recent development, but even back in the 1920s, people were playing pranks for audiences. Later on, the idea of pranking moved to television. *Candid Camera* originally started out as a radio show called *Candid Microphone*, then moved to TV in 1948. Unsuspecting people were put in embarrassing, confusing, or humorous situations while their reactions were recorded. When they were finally let in on the joke, they would hear the show's catchphrase: *Smile, you're on Candid Camera.*

Survivor gave audiences a glimpse into how other people think and behave, both on camera and when they think others aren't watching. A large cash prize at the end upped the stakes. The first season's final episode had more than fifty million viewers. The show began its forty-seventh season in 2024.

Survivor was only one reality show that came out of the early 2000s. *Big Brother, The Bachelor, The Real Housewives, America's Next Top Model*, and *American Idol* were a few others. By 2024 around 80 percent of adults watched some form of reality TV.

American Idol **viewers watched their favorite singers compete for prizes of money and a record deal.**

Rogan (*right*) speaks with the wrestler Test during a special *Fear Factor* episode featuring WWE stars.

Unlike some reality TV that featured the same pool of competitors all season, each episode of *Fear Factor* had six new contestants. They were challenged to compete in three different stunts for the chance to win up to $50,000. The network had their idea. But now the show needed a host—one with a charismatic personality, physical strength, and a strong stomach. Rogan seemed like the perfect fit.

Rogan didn't think the show would last more than a couple episodes. He only signed on because he thought it would boost his stand-up career. But the show wasn't canceled right away. *Fear Factor* originally ran for six seasons, from 2001 to 2005—each season taking more risks than the last.

At first the stunts that contestants had to endure were things like eating bugs, being covered by rats, or jumping from tall heights. But later seasons forced them to eat increasingly gross animal parts, run into burning buildings, or attempt to escape from plexiglass boxes as they dangled from helicopters. Rogan began hating coming to work. Watching desperate people do things for money made him sick to his stomach. He did return to host a final season in 2011. He did it for the money but immediately regretted it.

Being a reality show host was hard. It got Rogan more work, though. In 2003 Adam Carolla and Jimmy Kimmel left *The Man Show*, a satirical comedy program, and Rogan and fellow comedian Doug Stanhope were hired as their replacements. The gig didn't last long, but Rogan

Comedians Jimmy Kimmel (*left*) and Adam Carolla hosted *The Man Show* from 1999 to 2003.

had already mentally moved on. He continued to work on his stand-up and hired camerapeople to follow him on the road for *JoeShow*, a web series he used to release comedy clips. He also recorded full-length comedy specials and made guest appearances on a variety of TV shows and movies.

Rogan's personal life was also taking off. He had met Jessica Ditzel in the early 2000s, and they married in 2009. Their daughters, Lola and Rosy, were born in 2008 and 2010. Rogan adopted Ditzel's daughter, Kayja Rose, as well. The rest of the family stays relatively private, letting Rogan shine brightly in the spotlight.

Rogan (*right*) and his wife, Jessica Ditzel, attend an F1 Grand Prix race in Austin, Texas, in 2024.

PODCASTING

Rogan had been on TV, in movies, and behind-the-scenes in the fighting world. On December 24, 2009, he added *podcaster* to his résumé when *The Joe Rogan Experience* launched its first episode. Comedian Brian Redban was the show's producer and co-host. The idea was that Rogan and Redban would sit down and chat about whatever came to mind. That year, it is estimated that more than twenty thousand new podcasts were published. By August 2010 Rogan's had reached the Top 100 iTunes podcasts. People could watch live on Ustream, although eventually the show moved to YouTube. Episodes lasted between two and three hours, with the longest episode coming in at five hours and nineteen minutes long. Other podcasts typically ranged from ten minutes to an hour in length. The fact that Rogan's episodes were so long spoke to his ability to listen to his guests and engage audiences.

Redban was technically the podcast's first guest. Episode three featured their first outside guest, comedian Ari Shaffir. At first their guests were mostly comedians, such as Tom Segura, John Heffron, and Bill Burr, or martial artists, like Eddie Bravo or Mayhem Miller. Rogan knew keeping a consistent schedule with fresh information was important to earning and keeping fans. Typical podcasts only last for six months before either the host or the audience lose interest. Rogan's guest list expanded to include experts in subjects as wide as law, music, writing, and science.

Rogan invited politicians, businesspeople, and

The History of Podcasting

Telling stories and listening to other people is both the oldest type of historical record and the most modern. Ancient people passed information on to the next generation through stories and songs. People today use recording devices to preserve that information for anyone who may be interested.

Online radio stations started popping up in the 1990s but didn't fully take off until faster broadband internet in the 2000s made streaming easier. People could suddenly listen to the radio anywhere, and creators could combine music or talk shows with visual art or text. And the best part was that anyone could make these audio blog posts!

There wasn't a way to easily upload or download files. In 2003 David Winer and Christopher Lydon invented a way to download audio blog posts to computers or mobile devices. A year later the word *podcast* was born. By 2005 the music sharing platform iTunes offered support for podcasts, allowing users to subscribe, download, and manage around three thousand free podcasts. By 2025 there were up to four million podcasts available on all platforms.

In 2005 people used iPods to listen to podcasts.

magicians. “I only have people on the show that I’m genuinely interested in talking to,” Rogan said. “I never do a podcast just because a person is popular. It’s always from a place of ‘I think it would be cool to talk to that person.’”

Rogan let guests talk about whatever they wanted, and the dialogue flowed naturally. Sometimes, the guest’s area of expertise wasn’t explored at all. It wasn’t ignored–it just never made it into the conversation. Kat Rosenfield, a culture writer and novelist, commented on Rogan’s ability to listen. “He is very naturally curious. He wants to ask questions,” she said. “He wants to know what’s up with his guests and he has good instincts to make it an engaging listen.” And people liked to listen to Rogan listening. By October 2015 *The Joe Rogan Experience* was being downloaded sixteen million times a month.

His innate curiosity and the growing popularity of *The Joe Rogan Experience* led to more opportunities for Rogan to gain new skills and advance his career. In 2013 Rogan and fellow comic Duncan Trussell hosted *Joe Rogan Questions Everything*, an investigative TV series. For six episodes they explored legendary creatures called cryptids, psychic abilities, and UFOs. Rogan also recorded more stand-up specials and continued announcing UFC fights. He earned a black belt in Brazilian jiujitsu and 10th Planet Jiu Jitsu, a nontraditional form of the sport founded by Eddie Bravo.

Rogan signed a licensing deal with Spotify in September 2020. The audio platform paid $200 million

The Joe Rogan Experience **signed an exclusive deal with Spotify in September 2020.**

for exclusive rights to the world's most-streamed podcast. That May Rogan moved his family from California, where they had lived for twenty-five years, to Austin, Texas. It was early in the COVID-19 pandemic, and Rogan felt California's health and safety restrictions, which included stay-at-home orders and mask mandates, were extreme. He bought a $14.4 million-dollar lakeshore home, complete with a cutting-edge recording studio. In his mansion he could live, work, and play by his own rules.

CONTROVERSIES

Rogan had millions of podcast listeners, and the number just kept growing. Between September 2020 and December 2021, the show's listener base grew by 75 percent. The show was no stranger to controversy, though. In April 2021 Spotify removed forty-two past episodes of *The Joe Rogan Experience* due to controversial guests and topics. Discussions in the podcasts included instances of transphobia, sexual harassment of a minor, white supremacy, and antisemitism. People were upset. They felt like having guests with those beliefs on his podcast made what they said seem acceptable and okay to repeat.

Rogan's cross-country pandemic move wasn't the only COVID-related thing that caught the public's eye. In December 2021 Rogan had Dr. Robert Malone, a scientist critical of vaccines, on his podcast. Malone made multiple claims that had already been proven false. Rogan had already given his opinion on the pandemic, claiming that young and healthy people didn't need to be vaccinated. He also suggested a drug to treat parasites could be used to treat COVID. More than one thousand doctors, medical workers, and scientific experts signed an open letter to Spotify speaking out against the anti-vaccine rhetoric. Rhetoric is language designed to be persuasive or appealing to its listeners. By giving Malone—and other COVID-deniers—equal airtime as other doctors and medical professionals, Rogan seemed to be presenting the anti-vaccine rhetoric as science-backed evidence. The medical professionals who signed the letter did not want Rogan removed from the platform. Instead, they asked for more moderation against false information.

Medical professionals weren't the only ones to speak out against *The Joe Rogan Experience*. Other celebrities and podcasters began to pull their content from Spotify and call for a boycott of the app. Neil Young, Joni Mitchell, Brené Brown, and India Arie were only some of the artists who pulled their music and podcasts from Spotify. They didn't want their work to share space with the misinformation being spread by Rogan's

Dr. Robert Malone is both a scientist who studies viruses and a vaccine skeptic.

Musician Neil Young temporarily pulled his music from Spotify to protest sharing the platform with Rogan.

podcast. Spotify employees threatened to strike or quit, too. In response Spotify vowed to stop the spread of COVID misinformation. They posted links to the app's COVID-19 hub, flagged any episodes that mentioned the pandemic with a content advisory tab, and added a disclaimer statement before each episode. Rogan released a ten-minute video promising his podcast would be more balanced.

But the controversy wasn't over yet. In February 2022 a video circulated on social media. It contained clips of more than twenty incidents where Rogan used inappropriate slurs or made hurtful, racist statements on his podcast. After that, Spotify removed another 113 episodes from *The Joe Rogan Experience* library. Rogan selected seventy of them himself. Daniel Ek, the CEO of Spotify, also pledged to invest $100 million over time to help produce and develop music and podcasts from marginalized groups. Rogan stood by his podcast, though. "I'm not trying to promote misinformation, I'm not trying to be controversial," he said. "I've never tried to do anything with this podcast other than to just talk to people."

Shock Jocks

Broadcasters who say or do provocative or controversial things are called shock jocks. America's first shock jock was Joe Pyne, a polarizing figure in the 1960s. Pyne was not above baiting guests into shouting matches, and, at its height, *The Joe Pyne Show* had ten million people tuning in every week.

Some argue that Rogan isn't a shock jock because he's not the one saying the controversial things—he usually lets his guests say them. Generally, interviews on Rogan's show are low-key and rarely heated. However, he has also not shied away from problematic topics or staying out of the media spotlight.

Rogan endorsed candidate Bernie Sanders in the 2020 US presidential election.

TALKING POLITICS

Rogan wasn't afraid to discuss any topic, whether it was a global pandemic or United States politics. Most of his listeners are young and male—his audience is around 80 percent men, half between the ages of eighteen and thirty-four. Many of them trust Rogan more than mainstream media. During the 2020 presidential election, Rogan endorsed Vermont senator Bernie Sanders for president after Sanders appeared on *The Joe Rogan*

Experience. Rogan said he admired Sanders for his strong convictions and consistency in politics. Some people were upset. They felt that Rogan's history of transphobia, antisemitism, misogyny, pandemic denial, and controversial interviews didn't align with this endorsement. But others hoped Rogan's endorsement would encourage potential voters to get to the polls. Rogan also had additional presidential hopefuls Tulsi Gabbard and Andrew Yang on as guests. Three other candidates—Joe Biden, Pete Buttigieg, and Elizabeth Warren—had approached Rogan for interviews as well. However, Rogan refused to extend invites. He said he wasn't interested in having a conversation with them.

In June 2022 Rogan praised Florida governor Ron DeSantis as a potential presidential candidate. He felt DeSantis's handling of COVID—resisting lockdown measures and shrugging off vaccine mandates—had been good moves. Like Rogan, DeSantis had promoted untested medical treatments. However, DeSantis dropped out of the presidential race in January 2024. In August of the same year, Rogan expressed his support for Robert F. Kennedy Jr., also known as RFK Jr., who had been a podcast guest in 2023. Rogan said RFK Jr. was the only candidate who made sense to him, although he later clarified that it wasn't an official endorsement.

Republican candidate Donald Trump wasn't a fan of Rogan's choice in candidates. In 2022 Rogan had said he wouldn't have Trump on the podcast. He called him a threat to democracy. Two years later, after Rogan shared his support for RFK Jr., Trump challenged Rogan in an online post. Rogan finally relented to having Trump on his show. Trump sat in the podcast's guest seat on October 25, 2024. Afterward—and hours before election day—Rogan finally endorsed Trump. Did Rogan and other podcasters change the election's outcome? No one can be totally sure, but experts can agree that podcasts shaped the way the race was won.

Read the Headline

For a long time people had to wait for their morning newspaper to show up on their doorstep to see what was going on in the world. Today, 86 percent of Americans get their news from their phones, tablets, or computers. Only 5 percent would rather read the news in a physical paper. Anywhere from 19 to 31 percent of people find their news on social media, and between 9 and 21 percent of people get their news from podcasts. These numbers are always changing, though, and are sometimes hard to track. For example, in 2024, anywhere from 17 to 35 percent of people got their news from TikTok. But those stats are for adults over eighteen. The number of users seventeen and younger could be much higher.

TO THE MOTHERSHIP

When Rogan bought his house and moved to Texas, he also bought a comedy club. The venue was originally for movies. It was the first movie theater in Austin. Over the years its doors have welcomed theatrical shows, musicians, and films. Its last owner, the Alamo Drafthouse, closed in 2021 due to the pandemic. Rogan bought it the following year and turned it into Comedy Mothership, a comedy club and bar. The club, which opened its doors in March 2023, has two rooms named after the atomic bombs that were dropped on Japan at the

Rogan's comedy club, Comedy Mothership, is located in downtown Austin, Texas.

end of World War II. The décor is alien-themed, with a huge UFO at the club's entrance, and heavily inspired by The Comedy Store, the Hollywood club where Rogan got his start.

Rogan wasn't the only comedian to move to Texas. Others have made their way from Los Angeles to Austin. Some left for the same reason Rogan did—looser restrictions, both socially and politically. Others came seeking a more affordable place to live. Rogan's club has given all of them a venue close to home. The city's central location makes it easy for comedians on either coast to easily fly in, too. During Comedy Mothership's opening night, famous comedians joined Rogan onstage. Rogan celebrated the fact that he couldn't be fired from his own club while he spoke out against cancel culture.

THE FUTURE

In February 2024 Rogan and Spotify renegotiated his contract. *The Joe Rogan Experience* would no longer be exclusive to Spotify. It became available on Apple Podcasts, Amazon, and YouTube as well. The deal, worth $250 million, also gave Rogan a share of ad revenue. That year *The Joe Rogan Experience* was the number one podcast on Spotify for the fourth year in a row.

Rogan continues to make appearances as a UFC commentator, but the podcast is his biggest claim to fame. As of the beginning of 2025, he had recorded 2,495 podcasts for a total of 6,599 hours, or 275 days'

Health and Wellness

In 2011 Rogan founded a supplement and fitness company called Onnit with YouTuber Aubrey Marcus. Onnit sold workout supplements and routines, oil, clothing, and fitness programs. They also sold Rogan's e-book *The Facts of Life with Joe Rogan*, which was full of life lessons Rogan had learned over his career.

Aubrey Marcus founded the fitness company Onnit with Rogan.

The thing that sold Rogan on the company was its use of brain-boosting substances called nootropics. There are many different types of nootropics; some are actual drugs, such as Adderall, while others, such as ginger or caffeine, are available over the counter. The use of nootropics is controversial. But Rogan liked what he saw and felt nootropics would help him stay sharp when he called UFC games. Onnit was sold to Unilever in 2021.

In 2024 Onnit was sued over misleading advertising. Its Alpha BRAIN supplement claimed to support memory, focus, and processing speed, even though the clinic trial by the company didn't prove any of that. The lawsuit said that Alpha BRAIN was little more than a placebo. In tests there was little evidence that it worked. In fact, sometimes people who took an actual placebo performed better than those who took Alpha BRAIN. Although Rogan was no longer the company owner and not named in the lawsuit, he continued to promote Alpha BRAIN heavily on his podcast.

Rogan is outspoken on his podcasts, in his comedy clubs, and in the UFC ring.

worth of content. There have been 1,153 different guest appearances, with martial artists Brendan Schaub and Eddie Bravo topping the appearance chart with ninety-three and eighty-nine drop-ins, respectively. The podcast had been viewed on YouTube around 410 million times. The most watched episode is Elon Musk's appearance in 2018. It has been viewed almost sixty-nine million times.

Rogan continues to perform stand-up as well. His seventh comedy special, *Joe Rogan: Burn the Boats*, was released in August 2024. He also announced plans to expand the Comedy Mothership. He wants to include a theater, a second club, and a comedy festival held in Austin with the biggest names in comedy making appearances.

Rogan's voice has a wide reach and has changed the way media is consumed in America. The importance of connecting with an audience, listening to what other people have to say, and speaking your mind are all part of that legacy. Podcasts come and go, but the impact of *The Joe Rogan Experience* will remain for years to come.

IMPORTANT DATES

1967 Joseph James Rogan is born in Newark, New Jersey.

1988 Rogan performs his first stand-up show.

1994 *Hardball* premieres on network television.

1997 Rogan makes his first appearance as a UFC commentator.

1999 Rogan records *I'm Gonna Be Dead Someday*, his first stand-up show.

2001 The first season of *Fear Factor* airs.

2009 The first episode of *The Joe Rogan Experience* launches.

2011 Rogan and Aubrey Marcus found Onnit.

2015 *The Joe Rogan Experience* is being downloaded sixteen million times per month.

2020 Rogan and Spotify sign an exclusive licensing deal worth $200 million.

2021 Dr. Robert Malone appears on *The Joe Rogan Experience*, prompting a letter to Spotify from hundreds of medical professionals.

2023 Comedy Mothership opens its doors.

2024 Rogan and Spotify agree on a $250 million streaming deal.

Joe Rogan: Burn the Boats premieres on Netflix.

Donald Trump is a guest on *The Joe Rogan Experience*.

SOURCE NOTES

7 Joe Rogan, "Joe Rogan Experience #2219 – Donald Trump," *The Joe Rogan Experience*, October 25, 2024, https://www.youtube.com/watch?v=hBMoPUAeLnY.

8 Joe Rogan, "Joe Rogan Experience #2219 – Donald Trump," *The Joe Rogan Experience*, October 25, 2024, https://www.youtube.com/watch?v=hBMoPUAeLnY.

9 Adam Wren, "Who Won the Day? Joe Rogan," *Politico*, October 31, 2024, https://www.politico.com/live-updates/2024/10/31/2024-elections-live-coverage-updates-analysis/who-won-the-day-00186686.

9 Joe Rogan, "Joe Rogan on Growing Up Without a Dad," JRE Clips, October 20, 2018, https://www.youtube.com/watch?v=5HfywG4bGs

19 Joe Rogan, "How Joe Rogan Got Into the UFC," JRE Clips, February 4, 2019, https://www.youtube.com/watch?v=5HfywG4bGsI.

27 "The Art of Podcasting with Joe Rogan and His New Multiyear Spotify Partnership," Spotify: For the Record, February 2, 2024, https://newsroom.spotify.com/2024-02-02/the-art-of-podcasting-with-joe-rogan-and-his-new-multiyear-spotify-partnership/.

27 Sam Cabral, "Joe Rogan's Path to a Once-Improbable Trump Interview," *BBC*, October 25, 2024, https://www.bbc.com/news/articles/cjr4dnv91p7o.

32 Sam Shead, "Spotify CEO Apologizes to Staff for Joe Rogan Controversy as Episodes Get Removed," CNBC, February 7, 2022, https://www.cnbc.com/2022/02/07/spotify-ceo-apologizes-to-staff-for-joe-rogan-issue-episodes-get-removed.html.

LEARN MORE

Britannica Kids: COVID-19
https://kids.britannica.com/students/article/COVID-19/634816

Britannica Kids: Mixed Martial Arts (MMA)
https://kids.britannica.com/students/article/mixed-martial-arts-MMA/626791

Edwards, Sue Bradford. *Making Podcasts*. Essential Library, 2025.

Krohn, Frazer Andrew. *MMA: UFC Unleashed*. Abdo Publishing, 2023.

Leed, Percy. *Donald Trump: Unprecedented Politician*. Lerner Publications, 2025.

NPR: Starting Your Podcast: A Guide for Students
https://www.npr.org/2018/11/15/662070097/starting-your-podcast-a-guide-for-students

SELECTED BIBLIOGRAPHY

Deggans, Eric, "Spotify Keeps Joe Rogan's Podcast After Clips of Racist Slurs in His Episodes Surface," NPR, February 7, 2022, https://www.npr.org/2022/02/07/1078929975/spotify-keeps-joe-rogans-podcast-after-clips-of-racist-slurs-in-his-episodes-sur.

Gold, Michael, Tim Balk and Simon J. Levien, "6 Takeaways From Donald Trump's 3-Hour Podcast With Joe Rogan," *The New York Times*, October 26, 2024, https://www.nytimes.com/2024/10/25/us/politics/trump-joe-rogan-podcast.html.

Gooding, Dan, "Trump Wins Over Swing Voters With Joe Rogan Interview: Analysis," *Newsweek*, October 28, 2024, https://www.newsweek.com/trump-joe-rogan-podcast-swing-voter-positive-1976171.

Lane, Lexi, "A Look Inside Joe Rogan's Career Over the Years," *Newsweek*, November 20, 2024, https://www.newsweek.com/entertainment/celebrity-news/joe-rogans-career-over-years-1989119.

Maruf, Ramishah and Brian Stelter, "Joe Rogan Apologizes After a Compilation of Him Using Racial Slurs Spreads," CNN Business, February 6, 2022, https://www.cnn.com/2022/02/05/media/joe-rogan-racial-slur-apology-india-arie/index.html.

Nawaz, Amna and Maea Lenei Buhre, "History of Reality TV and Impact on Society Chronicled in New Book 'Cue the Sun!'," *PBS News*, July 1, 2024, https://artscanvas.org/books/history-of-reality-tv-and-impact-on-society-chronicled-in-new-book-cue-the-sun.

Neath, Amelia, "Joe Rogan-Backed Pharma Company Sued for Peddling Health Supplements with 'False' Advertising," *The Independent*, May 20, 2024, https://www.the-independent.com/news/world/americas/onnit-sued-supplements-joe-rogan-b2548166.html.

Seitz-Wald, Alex, Henry J. Gomez and Natasha Korecki, “How Trump Won—and Harris Lost—the 2024 Election,” *NBC News*, November 7, 2024, https://www.nbcnews.com/politics/2024-election/how-trump-won-harris-lost-2024-election-rcna178840.

INDEX

PHOTO ACKNOWLEDGMENTS

Image credits: Stacy Revere/Getty Images, p. 2; Tom Szczerbowski/Getty Images, p. 6; CHIP SOMODEVILLA/Getty Images, p. 8; Jeff Bottari/Getty Images, pp. 10, 40; Magicpiano/Wikimedia Commons CC, p. 12; Araya Doheny/Stringer/Getty Images, p. 13; Carlo Allegri/Getty Images, p. 14; Holly Stein/Getty Images, p. 15; Otto Greule Jr/Stringer/Getty Images, p. 16; Vince Bucci/Stringer/Getty Images, p. 18; Denise Truscello/Getty Images, p. 19; Peter Kramer/Getty Images, p. 20; Kevin Winter/Getty Images, p. 21; Getty Images, p. 22; Scott Gries/Getty Images, p. 23; Mark Sutton/Getty Images, p. 24; Justin Sullivan/Getty Images, p. 26; LIONEL BONAVENTURE/Getty Images, p. 28; Anadolu/Getty Images, p. 30; Jo Hale/Getty Images, p. 31; Scott Eisen/Stringer/Getty Images, p. 33; eric laudonien/Shutterstock, p. 36; Rick Kern/Stringer/Getty Images, p. 38.

Cover Image: Stacy Revere/Getty Images